Table of Contents

Real Natural Manhood:

The Authentic Man's Guide
To Courageous Manhood
In The Modern World

by *Vincent Vinturi*

www.RealNaturalSeduction.com

What Is A Real Man?

The big question. Are you a real man? Am I a real man? WHO is a real man…?

Every man is a man because manhood is biological. By the time you reach your teenage years, you are sufficiently mature to mate with a female of your species. So as far as nature is concerned, you can make babies and perpetuate the human race. And that makes you a man!

But …merely the ability to plant a seed doesn't make you a REAL man. Because the concept of a "real man" consists of 2 parts. First you must be a man. Check. Second, you must be REAL! Only then can you be a "real man".

But the odds are really stacked against you ever realizing your potential. Because as soon as you step foot outside of the womb, everybody is tugging at you, trying to make you this way and that way. So naturally, you go astray from YOUR way. You lose touch with what is REAL and natural to YOU and adopt what is contrived and artificial. So you can be a man biologically, yet not be a real man in the fullest sense.

To be a real man means to drop all the crap that's been heaped upon you, and to reclaim your realness, your authenticity, your naturalness, your innocence. **And by walking your *own* path and speaking your *own* truth, all of your quintessentially male qualities will blossom <u>as a natural consequence.</u>**

You will begin to bloom with maturity, edge, charm, charisma, resourcefulness, awareness, strength, perseverance, gusto, unpredictability, courage. In fact, to go your own way requires tremendous courage to begin with.

So how do you do this? How do you reclaim your realness and fertilize the soil from which your masculine qualities grow?

...By doing what you want.

What Do I Want?

Everything depends upon this one thing: ask yourself, *"what do I want?"*

"What do I want?" Ask yourself now. Ask yourself later. Keep asking yourself, as often as possible, and continue asking for the rest of your life. You may be surprised to find that you're completely out of practice, and asking yourself what you want, much less answering it, is strangely difficult.

As a child, there was no question of doing anything OTHER than what you wanted. Can you fathom having done what somebody ELSE wanted when you were a child? Impossible!

Though you may think this is a simple enough question to ask yourself, the implications are really tremendous...

Because once you ask yourself what you want, you'll eventually come up with an answer. And once you come up with an answer, you have to go and do it. You do it immediately. You do it no matter the cost. You do it no matter what your friends think, what your parents think, what onlookers think, and most of all, what you, yourself, think. Because thinking is what got you fucked up in the first place! So thinking is out...

You are asking your *heart*, your *gut* ...NOT your mind!

Your mind only tells you what you SHOULD want, what you OUGHT to want, based on all the conditioning you've been given. It can only provide the *illusion* of true wanting because it is based on thought. So you know what you THINK you want. But it's not what you *really* want.

This isn't a play on words. It's an <u>observable</u> and existentially significant distinction for you to understand. What your heart tells you - call it intuition if you like - is often *very* different from what your head tells you.

Have you ever been 'stuck in your head'? Have you ever watched 'that guy' who just acts crazy and aloof and has fun and doesn't care what *anybody* thinks about him or what he's doing? You know, the guy who just can't seem to fit in with the rest of society or walk the 'conventional' path...?

Yet this is the kind of guy who lives with a heart full of priceless treasures and irreplaceable experiences. This is the kind of guy who women are drawn to like moths to a flame. And the kind of guy who other men want to befriend and earn respect from.

Becoming this kind of man is the inevitable, practical result of following your heart. And doing what you want is the source. It is the fountain of your masculinity. It is the foundation of a compelling man.

Consider this: why are women not attracted to 'nerds'? It's not because nerds are intelligent. Non-nerds are intelligent, too. It's because nerds carry all their intelligence in their *heads*. They live in their heads, they flow through life in their heads and they're utterly disconnected from their hearts and their lower centers.

Women, on the other hand, flow through the world in a deep partnership with their hearts. They cross-check with their minds but the heart has the finally say. As a result, women are more intuitive, more fluid, more open, more aware, more present and more dynamic than men, IN GENERAL.

If you live in your head, how can you possibly relate with a person's heart? And if you continue relating to others just on a 'head' level, your interactions will always remain superficial, sterile and dry. The real juice starts flowing when you begin to relate to others on the level of your heart and their hearts.

So from now on, you are to consult *your heart*! Then you do what it says. You may be surprised to see that little by little you find yourself coming alive, as if for the first time. You begin to come into a place of deep alignment, self-respect and self love. This is the day that your life really begins.

An example:

You hate your job. You want to quit. Your boss is an asshole. Your coworkers are dull. But you stay anyway. You stay because it's secure. It's miserable but secure. Security is always miserable. And misery is always secure. You can always count on it to be there. But you don't have the guts to leave your secure misery. And make no mistake about it, it takes guts.

Just remember…you're going to die. And you're wasting your time doing something you don't care about, just for a paycheck. What good, then, is your money? You have food on your table and furniture in your apartment but the master of the house is missing. You don't even have your own self! So WHO is the one getting a paycheck…?

You want to quit? You quit. Right now. What are you going to do for money? For Food? For Shelter?

You'll figure it out. Because you'll have to. You are a man. *A man is a desert rose that blooms in the rugged sand...*

Scare yourself. Shock yourself. Give yourself a challenge and walk along the razor's edge. This is the only way to ripen as a man because manhood flowers only in danger, in uncertainty, in risk. You will never feel alive until you throw off the wet blanket of security. Stop doing what you don't want to do this instant and move into the unknown with all the strength you have.

Another example:

Your friends are boring and they bring you down. You tell them wistfully how you want to go traveling and live on a beach making handmade hemp jewelry (or whatever gets you off). Maybe they laugh at you. Or they say "oh…that's cool..."

They thinly conceal their scorn. "Who do you think you are to abandon the secure, mundane misery that binds us both…?" They, of course, would like to do the same, but they don't have the minerals. At least, they *think* they don't.

If these are the kinds of friends you have, it's time to move on. Not that they're bad people, no. Not that you don't care about them. But whether they know it or not, they're keeping you small. And a friend who really cares about you will let you go if he knows he's holding you back from bigger things...

No need for a declaration of independence, a statement of intent or a fanfare goodbye. Just stop talking to them and calling them and messaging them online, and move on. Find the people who inspire you and befriend them. Learn from them. Aspire with them. And quit wasting your time on *anybody* who doesn't enrich your life and call you to a higher standard.

That includes your family. That includes your lovers. That includes everybody who wants to keep you keep from growing and from the life of adventure that is your birth right, whether they know it consciously or not.

A Man Is The Terms He Stands By

The practical result of doing what you want habitually is that you begin to develop terms, boundaries, preferences. You develop these terms out of your own life experiences. They are NOT rules given to you by somebody *else*. They are your own, freely chosen terms and they are deeply personal.

When you figure out that certain things make you feel like shit and certain things make you feel great about yourself, you'll tend to avoid the ones that make you feel badly. Not because somebody told you so or because you're 'supposed to'. Not because of some ideology you got from your parents or your priest. But simply because you go out into the world with your eyes open and pay attention to how you *really* feel about things.

In other words, you begin to live with awareness...

Awareness

Awareness is just like a candle.

In a dark room you can't see anything. You take your steps carefully because you might stub your toe on something. You're not sure where anything is, even if you've been in this room before. But when you bring a candle into a dark room you can *immediately* see the objects around you.

If somebody asks you to find a certain book in a dark room, and gives you detailed instructions on finding it; where the book is, about how heavy it is, what the cover feels like, how many steps to take to reach the bookshelf from the door, the thickness of the cover...

You MAY find the book in the dark but you wouldn't be 100% certain it's the right one. But with even the tiniest candle in your hand, you have enough light to find the book almost instantly AND to know *without a doubt* that it's the right one.

It's just like interacting with women. There are a million books, audio tapes,

DVDs, and seminars you can take that will teach you the formulas, steps, techniques, things to say and how to stand to be attractive to women. Yet with even the most detailed directions, you'll still be groping in the dark and uncertain about what you're doing, why you're doing it, where you're going and what exactly you're looking for. You'll still be pussyfooting around, afraid of tripping on something because you don't have a candle to light your way...

So I want you to understand that you do NOT need any more **directions**. You need LIGHT to see. And <u>awareness</u> is your light. With it, you'll be able to "see" through the darkness of *any* situation. Awareness means opening your eyes and looking at everything that happens in your life *directly*.

Every situation you encounter is unique and if you go in with rehearsed lines, formulas and techniques, you'll undermine your very ability to pay attention to the situation at hand, to see it for what it is, and to respond spontaneously, freshly and organically.

Work with what a situation gives you. Improvise. You don't need to be clever, you don't need to be rehearsed or prepared. Just be AWARE, and everything will flow from there. Trust in existence. Just by staying aware, you will learn things - intangible, ineffable things - that no book can impart to you.

As a beautiful Italian woman once told me "awareness is sexy." It is your light, and it will shine on those around you if you keep it burning. By bringing your awareness to each situation, you treat it with the uniqueness it deserves.

In so doing, you cultivate an uncanny, childlike sensitivity...

Sensitivity

Sensitivity is your capacity to feel and perceive. For instance, when you do a person wrong and see the hurt look on their face, and feel the feelings of self-disgust in your stomach, but ignore them, you put a lid on your sensitivity. The situation is right in front of your eyes. You know what's happening. You feel it. You see it. But you *choose* to escape it. It's too overwhelming to keep aware in the face of an action you didn't want to take. So you escape. This is escap*ism* but it is not escape.

If you are sensitive and courageous (and sensitivity REQUIRES courage), you will SEE the situation and what your actions do to you and to other people, and you'll allow yourself to feel it totally, fully.

In this state of sensitivity, you are better equipped to *respond* in a way that leaves you feeling good about *yourself*. That's not to say that you should be a people pleaser. But by cultivating sensitivity, you'll become more graceful at being yourself without negatively affecting others if you can help it. You'll develop a clarity about what you find acceptable for yourself and what you don't.

But let it be said that hurt feelings are part of life, and no matter how elegantly you conduct yourself, no matter how aware you are of your actions, people WILL get hurt, particularly when you're committed to walking down your own path at all costs. You will hurt your friends, you will hurt your lovers and you will hurt yourself, but you will grow more and more sensitive and learn from it. Just watch that you don't go on repeating the same mistakes over and over; that is simply stupidity.

But isn't doing what you want all the time selfish...?

Selfishness

Yes. Doing what you want all the time IS selfish. It's the very definition of selfishness. And there's absolutely nothing wrong in it. In fact, living selfishly takes tremendous courage, while living selflessly takes no courage at all. To grow, to evolve, to make a dent in the universe, requires that you be true to yourself in a world where being true to yourself is condemned, shamed, laughed at, punished.

Selfishness has been given a bad rap because it doesn't serve any of the vested interests. It doesn't serve any of the people who want to control your life. Selfishness serves you, the individual. It doesn't serve any collectivities, societies, cultures, power structures, politicians, corporations, churches, interest groups. It serves *you*.

But if you can be convinced, as most people have been at an early age, that selfishness is an evil, contempt-worthy quality, then naturally you feel guilty and shameful whenever you think selfish thoughts or behave selfishly. People 'tsk tsk' you for your selfishness. And you might even agree with them that you ARE a bad person for being so.damn.selfish.

But the truth is, *you must fill YOUR cup first before it can overflow to others.* It is the only way you can be of any use to yourself. And thus, it is the only way you can be of any use to others. If you have nothing to give, what can you offer to a lover, a colleague, a friend, a son, a father? If you constantly bend to others and sacrifice yourself for others, you will have no self respect. You will not even have any SELF!

It will be just as if you were to go on pouring the contents of your cup into dozens of other cups. Soon your cup empties and you have nothing more to pour. But if you stand at the source of existence and fill your cup, it will always fill up and overflow. Then others can come and put their cups under yours. Your cup will become like a spring, and provide nourishment for many others. And you will have done nothing except simply make sure that *your own* cup remained full...

So the idea of true selfishness - simple, innocent selfishness - has been tainted. Look at the word. Self-ish-ness... What it literally means ...is to be yourself! But you've been told your whole life to silence the still, small voice inside of you and to live according to others, by others and for others. For your parents, your teachers, your church, your community, your friends. For society, for the greater good, for mankind, for the environment, for the kids, for the polar bears. For everybody and anybody BUT yourself!

So the one man is living for the other man and neither man is living for himself. But this is just silly... Nobody knows better than you how to make you happy. So YOU are the best candidate for making your life look the way you want it to look. Should you be dependent on the good will of others to live FOR you? Will another man carry that torch and keep it burning with the same level of trust, caring and ownership as you...?

To be yourself means to spend quality time with yourself and to discover all of the hidden gems deep inside of you. If you don't go in, you'll never find these gems. But if you go in, you'll soon discover a brilliance shining within you that will fill you with such joy, that you'll naturally want to share it! In fact, you won't be able to NOT share it! Because gems can't help but reflect light and dazzle the eye...

This is what I call "overflowingness". It is the quality of being you have when you are in a deep alignment, a deep harmony with yourself and with existence. You are so full of a special something that it literally overflows to everybody around you. And they can literally feel it. This isn't some cooky, new-age talk. You've *already* met overflowing people before. You've felt their tremendous overflowingness as if it were spilling right out of them and unto you.

And perhaps you even wondered what their secret is...

Masculine Poetry

What makes a man compelling? It's not any one thing. It isn't even the combination of many things. It goes beyond. It's an aroma. It's a song. It's a poetry.

That's what men today are missing - a masculine poetry. A rugged grace. An existential poise. Today's man lives up in his head or down in his pants, and the whole in-between is missing. Poetry requires flow, originality, dignity, know-how, inspiration, rhythm, heart.

What if everything you did, you did with your poetry? What if you suddenly become aware of the way you move, the way you speak, the way you interact with others? What if you brought your awareness and presence into every room you entered, every kiss you gave, every story you told? Do you think that perhaps this could change your life and the way you interact with people...?

Knowledge vs Knowing

Knowledge you have plenty of. It's crammed into your head like twinkie filling, and about as useful. Knowledge by its very nature is borrowed. It doesn't come from your direct experience. It comes out of other peoples' mouths and from books and from parents and from teachers. It's second-hand...

You know how many books exist on Amazon alone about dating, seduction and manhood? Tens of thousands. Go buy them! Put them on your shelf. Stuff them into your Kindle so you're always carrying around "the answer", "the technique". You can even read it all. But it won't make you a real man.

Knowledge is comforting. It exonerates you of responsibility. It relieves you of the necessity to treat every moment as unique, every person and situation as unique, and most of all, it frees you from the responsibility of bringing your own awareness and watchfulness into each situation. Hence the existence of 'self-help junkies'...

Knowledge is like a key. And every moment that existence gives you is a unique lock. But you have just the one key. It can't fit all the locks. You can jam this key into a lock, and *maybe* with enough torque and force you'll jimmy it open. But it will never open the lock like a key made just for that lock. Only your awareness can work that kind of magic.

It's only by embracing the uncertainty of a situation and actively bringing your awareness to the table that you will find all the resourcefulness, charm, humor, grace, beauty that you've had inside you all along. Through awareness, you will flower. Through awareness, you'll be able to drop your dependence upon theoretical knowledge and come to a deep, existential KNOWING.

The End of Self Help

Self-help is a ridiculously profitable industry that often thrives on selling people solutions to imaginary problems. But I say, **you don't need any more help**. The well intentioned fools have 'helped' you enough.

Inside of you this very moment, is contained ALL the strength, all the resourcefulness, and all of the attractive qualities that you've been seeking in books and DVDs and seminars. But these are all your *intrinsic qualities!* There can be no question of a book or a person or a seminar delivering them to you. The question is how to *rediscover* them and begin to share them with the world again.

Don't get me wrong, it's good to educate yourself and continue learning and growing. Just be careful of becoming a walking self-help encyclopedia who can recite all the answers to life's questions but lives his *actual* life in misery...

You are born a blank slate, a *tabula rasa.* But before you've even had a chance to experience anything of life <u>directly</u>, to do any thinking for yourself -- the do gooders are already stuffing you full of garbage ideas.

The ideas put into your head at this tender stage undermine your incredible intelligence and harden your heart. And unless you can drop them, they will ruin your life. All you need to do is take one honest look at the people around you.

Just look at them. Look how many of them are living in their own mental prisons with no idea of how to escape. Maybe you're even one of them.

So how do you get back to the source? To the happiness you had as a kid? How do you reclaim your adventurous spirit, your thirst for every drop of experience and the very thing you're born with -- overflowingness?

Start by showing up and stepping into the foreground...

Destined For The Foreground

Imagine you're on a stage. Like any stage, there is a background and a foreground.

The background is safe. It's dimly lit. You can stand silently in the background, and unless somebody is *really* paying attention, they may not even notice that you're there at all...

This is where you, like many men, *could* wind up standing nearly your whole life. In rare spouts of courage (or foolishness), you venture across the line where the light illuminates your body. And suddenly, the audience can see you. Now there can be no doubt that there really IS somebody on the stage. He was just hiding in the background until now...

As you inch slowly towards the front of the stage, you notice that the foreground is terribly bright, almost blinding. You can't even see the audience but you can *feel* them sitting there, watching. The light is hot and you perspire. The people in the audience can see your every pore dripping with nervous sweat and you wish you had makeup or a mask on so they couldn't see quite so clearly that you aren't *really* an actor, but just another person.

Unaccustomed to so many eyes on you and not prepared with so much as a third rate monologue, you are gripped by fear. What will you say to these people? You have absolutely nothing to say. Nothing rehearsed; nothing memorized, just plain nothing. You haven't even bothered to choreograph a little jig so that at least the audience will be a bit entertained; that they got their money's worth.

And now you have a choice…

You can CHOOSE to stay in the foreground and wing it, or you can retreat back into the shadows. You can choose: to write a song as you sing it, to pen a poem as you speak it, to create a dance as you dance it. And who knows if people will like it or not? They may even walk out of the theatre in droves, grumbling something about getting their money back.

But...you may find that as you dance your awkward new dance, your anxiety slowly fades. Your skin flows with sweat - yes! - but you're too busy having a blast to notice. Actually ...it feels kind of good! Then you *really* get into the swing of things. And your movements become more and more graceful, unselfconscious, lithe.

Some of the stragglers from the annoyed, departing audience hear the clopping of your feet on the wooden proscenium and turn their heads out of curiosity. What they see is a mad man dancing like he's possessed, splashing sweat everywhere with eyes closed. A man totally unaware that at any minute he may slip on his own sweat and go flying right off the stage! And naturally, madness of any kind is always amusing to watch.

"Is this part of the show?" one asks. "What the hell..." mutters another "this wasn't in the program!" "I know!" a third lights up, "this was the plan from the very beginning. To pretend to bore us and then bring this guy on stage for the punchline ...BRAVO!!!" The theatre slowly fills up again. But you don't notice. You're too busy dancing like Zorba The Greek.

And all it took to fill the theatre back up was the courage to be naked in front of others. To be totally scared yet stay in the foreground anyway. It took facing the audience to forget all about them. A paradox... Or is it? And in time, the fear you feel is less noticeable. It's still there, sure, and it comes back acutely from time to time. But that's the name of the game.

So you decide – with each new moment **you decide** – to STAY in the foreground. Because now you know for certain, you are NOT destined for the background. There's nothing there for you but darkness and ennui. Watching the action from backstage but not participating in it...? Nah, you're not interested in that. YOU are the lead in the play of your life. Though it's yours, even YOU can't predict what will happen in the next act - what to say about the finale!?

All the world's a stage. And you are destined for the foreground...

Everything You Know Is A Lie

Everything you know is a lie. Everything you've been taught by your parents, by your teachers, by the media, by your church/synagogue/temple, by your culture and society -- they're all lies.

Lies so clever and well camouflaged, that you've mistaken them for truth your whole life. But just like Neo's character in the movie *The Matrix*, you can vaguely feel that something is amiss, although you can't *quite* put your finger on it.

And what it comes down to is that you've never lived according to yourself. You haven't been given the chance! To live according to yourself and to follow your heart at all costs is frowned upon from every corner.

You're expected to be a good member of society, a good worker, a good son, a good father. But have you ever wondered why what defines 'good' is always coming from outside of you? And the guidelines to be 'good' are so varied and conflicting, that most men live their lives in a state of chronic, low-level anxiety and cognitive dissonance.

After all, how can you possibly reconcile being a good son with doing something your father totally disapproves of? Or how can you reconcile being a good worker with the overwhelming urge to quit your job and travel the world? And what to say about being a good member of society...? *Which* society? They're all different!

Family

Family deserves a special mention because it enjoys a very similar status to religion. But it's worse in many ways because it goes unquestioned. At least most people who have thought about religion critically have concluded, if silently, that *religion as such* is hogwash. A series of lies designed to scare you into submission and make you a good sheep that can be herded into a house of extortion every Sunday morning.

Religious ideology is a way to avoid living by giving you a superficial comfort with death. I say 'superficial' because this comfort is just intellectual, theoretical. You don't *know* it, you think it. It requires faith, belief. It is religion but it is not religiousNESS. It is doctrine. It does not arise out of *your own experience*.

Real comfort with death is *existential*. It comes from living your life so totally, so intensely and so joyfully, that even death, when it comes, is a celebration. Real comfort with death is something you feel in your heart. So it requires no faith, no belief. The only things that require you to *believe* in them or *have faith* in them are the things that don't exist. Real things are right in front of your eyes. They can be seen, heard, tasted, smelled and FELT deep inside of you.

Yet the family is blindly sanctified in much the same way as religion. Very few people question the sanctity of the family. Even though, most people don't like their families. *They're actually sick of them.* They're sick of the emotional blackmail they put each through. They're sick of the manipulation, the prostitution, the compromises of integrity. They say "I love you" and they mean "I can't stand you." They say "I miss you" and they mean "I wish I never had to see your face again!"

And when a man has these kinds of thoughts, he feels such guilt and shame that he could even THINK such a thing, that he represses it until it becomes a festering wound deep inside of him.

But parents aren't bad people. Like most other parents, your parents likely think you are 'theirs'. That you belong to them. That you should copy THEM, make THEM proud and be a good son to THEM. Anything you do which gratifies their egos will be rewarded and everything that stings their egos will be punished.

After all, they want to be able to say that "MY son is a success", "MY son is a straight A student" (ever see those bumper stickers?), "MY son is marrying that pretty girl and they'll give ME beautiful grandkids." Who is it all about...*you* or their 'son'?

It's true: you came through the parents. But you do not *belong* to them. Nor do you owe them anything. You are not obligated to them. Let me repeat, you do not owe your parents anything.

Yes, they've probably done a lot for you; an incomprehensible amount. But did they do it so they could come back to you and demand you sacrifice yourself in their service? Is that why they brought you into this life and gave you what they did...just as a 'favor' to obligate you?

Obligations are ugly. But commitments are beautiful. Obligations are extorted, forced, unasked for. Commitments are chosen, welcomed, earned. Your parents brought you into the world, provided for you and raised you. It may have felt like an obligation on their part if they thought they were being virtuous by sacrificing their lives for their children. (And all sacrifice breeds resentment in the heart of the person sacrificing.) Or it may have been a commitment that they freely undertook. Or it could have been a combination of both...

Either way, should their bringing you into the world make you eternally beholden to them? Enslaved to them? Forced to live according to them and for them? Parents are merely vessels, caretakers. It must be so, because the human child is utterly helpless. So dependance upon the parents is a survival necessity. But ...you are not their belonging. You do not belong to anybody because free human beings cannot possess one another. You are a part of the same existence as they are, as we all are. So there can be no question of belonging *to* someone. There is only a belonging *with* the universe.

So naturally, most people come to deeply resent their parents. And the vast majority of the world has 'mother issues' and 'father issues'. And it's inevitable. Here these people give birth to a person without his permission into a situation over which he has ZERO control and about which he has no say. They raise him so ineptly that he's left with a mountain of 'issues' to hash out, perhaps on a psychiatrist's couch. They make demands on him, thrust expectations upon him and all in the name of that beautiful word 'love'.

...Even though everybody knows deep down that true love knows nothing of expectation, demands or obligations. True love gives total freedom...

So it's only natural to point your finger at these people and blame them for the state of your life. But it's not your fault and it's not their fault. It's nobody's fault because biology is blind. It's bound to happen this way.

Yet even when certain members of your family make you miserable, you stick around. You stick around because you can get something. In fact, you stick around because you can LOSE something. What can you lose? Your security, your "Plan B", your option to have people to fall back on.

Perhaps you can get a bit of gift money on your birthdays, a place to stay and hot meals when you can't afford shelter, and other 'perks' for being part of the family. Even though you know perfectly well that sticking around in a situation that you don't want to be in - for ANY amount of security - is a treason against yourself that keeps you from blossoming as a man... It's just like a hard freeze before the fruit on a tree is about to ripen. It's *almost* ready to eat. But the freeze comes along and ruins the harvest.

And most men in this situation continue to prostitute themselves with a feeling of tremendous shame. They *know* they are avoiding the challenge of standing on their own two feet. And it IS a challenge. It is THE challenge. You can sit in the room where you grew up and have your mom do your laundry for you, OR ...you can answer the call of the unknown.

So the only way out of the feeling that your parents and family screwed you over without your permission is to go and live your life with total selfishness. To live it in danger and uncertainty, with no fall back plan. Even if it means going completely against your family's wishes. Go and do what you want right now, **today**. And drop every expectation others have of you, every obligation that you've undertaken unwillingly and every duty you've accepted reluctantly.

This is, in fact, the only way to eventually forgive and come to *love* your parents, or anybody else! Because when you live your life for other people, based on what *other* people want of you and expect of you, you betray yourself. You hear your heart's call but you ignore it. It's screaming at you. It's haunting you. But you stifle it. You turn a deaf ear. And because you're too scared to face it, you continue to compromise. You undermine your self. You become literally 'self-less'.

And if you don't even have your own self, what can you possibly share with somebody else...?

If you just walk into the darkness, even though you're afraid (and you WILL be afraid), you will come to flower as a man. Just by this very act. That's the way it goes. And when you flower as a man, your life becomes a rejoicing, a dancing, a poetry, a song. When you're overflowing with life and love and laughter, you will begin to feel a tremendous gratitude that you were put on this earth. You feel grateful for *everything* that has led you to such a beautiful life, **including your parents** with all their faults and mistakes. **Including your upbringing** with all its tragedies and miseries.

And from within this space, you can't help but feel great compassion for your parents. Because they likely behaved with you exactly the way their parents behaved with them. They were repeating. Merely acting out a script written by somebody else long ago, reciting bland, memorized lines and moving to ugly choreography. How can you feel anything but compassion for sleepwalking people who go on unknowingly knocking things over in the middle of their sleep?

And you, like the rest of us (to varying degrees), are a casualty of other people's sleep. But you can choose *away* from the hatred, the resentment, the victimhood, the hurting, the dwelling, the festering, . You can choose *towards* beauty, awareness, light, joy, adventure, freedom, LIFE!

You can choose...

The Illusion of Opposites

It may seem strange to you that I put words like 'danger and life', 'laughter and uncertainty', 'responsibility and freedom' in the same sentences. Because if you're out on your own, struggling to make your life work, and every moment is born out of uncertainty, how can there be laughter? If you're overloaded with responsibility, how can you have any freedom? And if you're living in danger, and your life can come to an end at any moment, how can you be living...?

To the logical mind, contradictions seem impossible. <u>But existentially, contradictions aren't contradictions, but compliments to one another.</u> They are just two sides of the same coin.

For instance, you get married to a woman. Now you both think that your commitment to one another has been affirmed, cemented. But in fact, there can now be NO commitment. You've involved the state and the church and the law and your families and your wedding guests into a private and sacred affair, and have asked them to put *their* seals of approval on *your* love. Which means you're unsure of your love. Otherwise, why should you need a contract binding you to stay together? What business does the law have in your love? Why is a priest - an intermediary - needed to give a blessing? Is not love a blessing straight from God?

The marriage in fact *destroys* your freely chosen commitment to love one another and replaces it with an ugly obligation. What was freely chosen before, is now tied up with the law, with the church, with your finances, with your possessions, with your reputation.

Inevitably, married couples begin taking each other for granted. Naturally! There's no more NEED to seduce one another afresh each day, to keep each other interested, to treat your lover as a newly born, evolving person with each moment that existence brings. It's signed, sealed and delivered. You're "married" and therefore, all of these things are *already* taken care of.

So while it MAY seem contradictory that commitment requires freedom, or that love requires non-attachment, the evidence from millions of married couples throughout the ages plainly shows them to be complimentary elements.

Likewise, a man cannot grow unless given a jolt, a challenge. You would think that the jolt would stunt his growth, but it actually spurs it on. You would think that by giving your lover the freedom to be with other men, she would lose love for you and run off with another. But because you respect her free will, her love for you has room to grow.

In Eastern spirituality, the ultimate state is enlightenment. Enlightenment is the transcendence of all dualities. Enlightenment is available to every man. You are potentially, or actually, an enlightened being. And all it starts with a little watching, a little noticing, a little understanding. And you will come to see that opposites always depend on each other. There is no light without darkness. No love without hate. No day without night. Existence has taken everything into consideration. And every moment you get is the precise moment you need when you get it.

Life Has Only One Direction: Forward

Whatever happened to you in your childhood. Whatever your parents and teachers and classmates did to you -- join the club. We're all damaged goods. But there's no more time to sit on a shrink's couch and unearth the past. It's gone.

And no matter how much your parents fucked you up, **every morning you wake up and you get to make a choice.**

You can *choose* what you want your next moment to look like. You can choose *in this very moment* how your life will play out. And the beauty is, you don't even have to think ahead. Nor do you need to think *back*. Because the NEXT moment always comes out of THIS moment. So if you bring all of your awareness, courage and strength to the NOW, the *next* now will take care of itself.

All of the planning, projecting, worrying you do; all of the ruminating and regretting about yesterday, is like a teleportation machine that *zaps* you out of the now. And the irony is that, as you're off in a tomorrow that doesn't exist or a yesterday that no longer exists, you are *still* in the now - but missing it completely! Even the future, when it comes, comes as a now.

And to interact with others in a way that captures their imagination and makes them feel present and alive around you, requires in the first place that you be there with them!

Give people the gift of presence. Because they're in the same situation. They've been taught the same crap of constant planning, constant worry, constant thinking about the past and the future.

Let your very presence be a magnet, keeping the people around you centered in the now, whether they like it or not. And many won't. Most people would rather live in their heads, missing the moment in its almost unbearable intensity. *It's easier to think about life than to experience it.* Thinking about life takes no guts, no effort. But to live takes passion.

So make love to life with all you've got, ravish it, have a here now love affair...

Here Now Love Affair

This moment is all you have. It's all you have because it's all that exists. Yesterday is gone. Tomorrow hasn't yet arrived. And tomorrow will NEVER arrive because when it does come, it will come as a 'now'! So the only place you can actually be, whether you know it or not, is here and now.

All the time you spend thinking about the past - what has been, what could've been, what should've been but wasn't - takes you out of the here and now. It takes you out of the here and now and places you there and then. So while your body is here and now, your mind is there and then. You have one foot in one world and another in a fantasy. So really, you are neither here nor there, neither then nor now. You are in a limbo.

When you begin to *really* live, your whole dedication, your love, your light, will shine in the here now. It's no coincidence that every Eastern religion has some sort of term for this state. Call it presence, awareness, watchfulness, absorption....

And living in the here now takes tremendous courage because it's an active, creative process. It means to continually burn the past and rise from its ashes like a phoenix. It means to let go of the reins of your illusory sense of control over the future and just bring your energies into the only moment you can control – this one.

Plunging yourself totally into THIS moment is also a practical thing. While you waste this moment planning for the future, you actually sabotage your future. Because the next moment ALWAYS come out of this very moment, and your life is nothing but a series of moments, strung together, one after the other.

Your charisma, your magnetism, your centering, your strength, ALL result from your presence in the here now. Logically so, because if YOU are not even here, WHO will be charming, charismatic, dynamic, etc.? He is off somewhere else... The person talking to you is talking to nothing but a body! His consciousness is out for a walk...

This takes a bit of practice... Every instant you can choose to live a little more here, a little more now, until you've got the hang of it most all of the time.

On Reclaiming The Manhood of Generations Past

In the 'men's community', you will find a lot of guys lamenting the fact that men have lost their manhood, their way. In essence, they've lost their masculinity. And a re-adoption of the things we used to believe in the 50's, for instance, or 20's, would rekindle the polarity between masculine earth and feminine sky.

But a longing for the past is always asking for trouble. For one, it's gone. Secondly, this is a different time, a different era, a different climate. So, it's time for a different man. A NEW man. Now is NOT the time for the man of the 50's or the 20's or whatever bygone era.

Rather than hearken back to some antiquated male archetypes, you are absolutely free to become not only your own man but your own KIND of man. There is no *universally* masculine man. While there are certainly 'alpha' traits that 'alpha men' across different cultures tend to exhibit, trying to cultivate them for their own sake can result in a lopsidedness.

This is why I show you a different way. A way of metaphor, suggestion, analogy, hinting. Because some things can't be conveyed directly. It's the difference between explaining to you the view from the beautiful mountaintop and *leading* you up there unsuspectingly, until you find yourself beholding the majestic view...

The True Meaning of Responsibility

Without freedom there can be no responsibility, nor without responsibility any freedom. But the word responsibility has been corrupted almost beyond recognition, to the point that most men cringe at the very word.

But if you look at the word, it breaks down into 'response' and 'ability'. So it is simply your ability to respond! Few people go about their lives responding. Most just react. They react like robots. In fact, the ONLY thing a robot can do is react. You give it a certain programming, and depending on the input, it produces a predictable output.

Most men live as robots for the simple reason that *men have not been taught how to watch.* By simply watching what happens within you and outside of you, you will notice a space growing between an 'input' and your 'output'. Because when you watch, you first see what is happening.

Watching is a receptive activity. Unlike interpretation, which is an active, aggressive force, watching requires you to suspend judgment. Because once you begin interpreting and judging, you are no longer watching. So by watching, you just *see it*. Whatever it is. **Then** you can *decide* how to respond. By watching, you give the moment room to *breathe* and time seems to come to a halt. Thus you cultivate an ability to respond and you become 'responsible.'

Responsibility does NOT mean that you take on obligations that you didn't ask for and don't want. That's duty – a true 4-letter word. And a man who loves himself rejects obligations thrust upon him unasked for and unwillingly. A responsible man takes on commitments that he *chooses* of his own free will because he wants to. He is free.

Only a free man can be responsible, and only a responsible man can be free. Because freedom is a great unknown. If you are truly free, then you go with existence and see what it brings you, and respond to IT. Even though you don't know what's coming next.

You're in suspense...

Keeping Yourself In Suspense

The more you simply notice what's happening inside you and around you, like a watcher on the hill, the less you'll get in your own way. As the ceaseless interpretations of your mind subside, you'll find that existence brings you moments and emotions that you would have missed if you had been busy interpreting. A certain suppleness arises in your being and you find yourself in utter suspense.

In short, you'll find that you don't know what's coming next. Because you're not following a rigid set of rules for conducting your life, but bringing your awareness to each situation. You don't even know *yourself* what you will feel, say or do next. You keep yourself in suspense.

This is an incredibly attractive way of flowing through the world. It means you don't cling. You don't hold grudges. You don't get hung up on the past. You sway. Even the tallest tree must sway with a strong wind. If it is rigid, it will be uprooted and destroyed. Likewise, the more you sway with the winds of life, the stronger and more resilient you become.

On Death And Dying

The big irony about death is that only the man who is not living fears it. His life is a dullness, a boredom, a predictability. Yet the prospect of dying terrifies him. Strange... here is is a man who isn't even living, who has nothing much to lose, but the thought of death causes him great fear.

The alive man, on the other hand, doesn't fear death. He *can't* fear death because he walks into it every day. This is a man who embraces uncertainty and danger. He goes bravely into it because in danger he feels alive. And though this man is in a great overflowingness, though he has *everything* to lose, death doesn't rattle him.

The truly alive man has come to feel a distinctly existential phenomenon: that if there is life in you, there can be no death. Death is merely the continuation of life; a moving of energy from one place to another. And when you're so full of gratitude and joy for every moment you've been given in THIS life, even death will be a cause for celebration.

In fact, when you live in the here and now and death comes knocking, what can you do but welcome it as you've courageously welcomed everything else existence has put before you? Only the escapist fears death. His cowardice haunts him even into his last moments. And in trying to escape death, even as he dies, he misses its tremendous beauty. A real man faces everything that comes, head-on. He is there, the moment is there. "So," he figures, "why not give it all I've got?"

No amount of clever writing will help you understand what I'm telling you here. It is not a thing that can be conveyed through words. It is *existential*. It is felt, observed and understood here in the real world. So if you want to stop living your life in fear of death, go bravely into the unknown with all your strength. Do it every day, all the time, and you'll come to appreciate that without the unknown, life could not be an adventure. And after all, what is death but the ultimate unknown and the greatest adventure?

Frolicking

Why are you not frolicking? Is not your life just one great playground? If it wasn't, why on earth would you even be here? Look at the dogs play, look at the kitties and cows and monkeys play. Are you so above them that you can't enjoy each moment the way they do?

Only humans are so silly to think we have some special, grand destiny on this earth. We get so serious about 'making an impact', 'leaving a mark'. Although *everybody* is forgotten with time... Even the most famous folks drop out of the history books eventually. And what good is it to have your name in a history book, anyway? Is it worth it to trade your life for some ink on a page that somebody may or may not ever read again?

Life has no purpose, no goal, no to-do list. It's a let-go. A frolicking.

The Law of Change and Letting Things Go

The first thing that children should be guided in understanding is the fundamental law of the universe: the law of change. The world is in a constant flux. That's what life is. Life is movement, flow, change, evolution, transformation. If it were complete, there would be nowhere left to go, nothing to improve upon. Nothing to discover, to learn, to explore.

We get it drilled into our heads that we can *force* a static state upon a dynamic existence. For instance, we think that by entering into *relationships*, we can freeze the process of *relating* to one another in that dreamy "honeymoon period". We think this imaginary structure is going to support our love and need to treat each other newly. But it's not a structure that supports, it's a cage that imprisons. And it's a prison of our own making.

Another example: a lover leaves us. The shock is too much. So we cling to her even harder. We hold on to her like a piece of flotsam in the middle of the ocean. We think we'll never meet somebody like her again. And that's true. But it's also true of the next person we meet. And the next. You'll never meet anybody like anybody else, ever.

And we know perfectly well that the clinging is unhealthy and doesn't put things as they were. And that's the mistake. Things were as they were. But now, they are as they are. If you spend this moment thinking about a past moment, you don't get the past moment back and you sleep through the present moment. It's lose/lose.

So focus on now. Watch the now. Go with life and everything it brings – the good, the bad, the ugly. Become *un*selective. Take it ALL in because it's ALL part of the whole. Go with the changes and watch them. And slowly, slowly, you will find your life turning into a great, epic story.

Women...

Man is one part, woman is the other part. The more you come into your own as a man, the more you'll find yourself longing to be surrounded by amazing women.

The feminine energy bolsters and supports the masculine energy. They compliment and feed each other. When you have inspiring women in your life, the things they'll teach you and the growth you'll go through, whether you like it or not, will be of profound proportions.

I wrote my first book - ***Real Natural Seduction: The Authentic Man's Guide To Meeting And Attracting Gorgeous Women Everywhere You Go*** – to deal specifically with the aspects of becoming effective with women. Because it's such an important part of becoming a man that it can't be simply left to chance.

However, there are a few things I didn't address regarding men and women in that first book that I know will be valuable to you...

Boldness

To be bold means to disregard any social conventions and ideas of appropriateness, and make a beeline for a cute girl, regardless of the situation. It means to take a chance even if you're scared and uncertain and have never been in this kind situation before.

You could be on the street, in the train, on a bus, at a family dinner. It really doesn't matter. It matters that you know what you want and you could give a damn what any on lookers think about it.

Interestingly, a club or bar scenario is *much* more nerve-wracking and high competition. It's the kind of venue that doesn't give you an inch and yet you get no extra love for approaching women in this environment.

But in the street, or any other *atypical* meeting place, women will often comment on how **bold** and ballsy it is of you to make a play. It's a mutually beneficial paradox. Your approach is easier. The woman thinks more of you. You don't spend a dime or unnecessarily frazzle your nerves at a bar or club. Win/win/win.

The reason most men don't approach women in these scenarios is because they think they shouldn't! So you have the added advantages of virtually zero competition and giving the girl a pleasant surprise.

But how do you give women a pleasant surprise each and every day...?

Seduce Each Other Every Day

There's a difference between relationships and relating. Relationships are stagnant, fixed, complete, dead. Once you're "in a relationship", you've already made "the deal". But human beings resent superimposed rules, restrictions and guidelines. We like freedom. That's why most relationships fail. Instead *...try relating.*

Relating depends not upon rules but upon your awareness. It depends upon you and your partner reinventing each moment you have together with freshness and excitement. It means to continue to seduce each other long after the "honeymoon period" is over. And it WILL be over sooner or later.

Of course, it's impossible to maintain the intrigue of that initial few weeks. You're on this intense dopamine kick and after a while it's bound to plateau. So your interest wanes. This is a pretty common (and natural) scenario for men. And it can be very difficult to reconcile this with a woman's desires, which tend to work in the exact opposite direction. Namely, women tend to go deeper and deeper into a relationship and get more interested in securing exclusivity and commitment from a man.

Nothing wrong with that. But from a psychological standpoint, women unconsciously categorize men into either the "provider" role or the "lover" role. And letting these roles blur too much is a bad idea...

You see, women have an innate need to secure a provider who has sufficient resources and who is tame and docile enough to pour his time and effort into raising offspring and establishing a comfortable 'home', rather than running around inseminating fertile wenches.

You can be either, or you can be both at different times in your life. But women find it very confusing if you try to be both at once. It's an evolutionary thing. So it's important to make these roles very clear. Do you want to be this woman's lover and ravish her for hours by candlelight? Or do you want to take her out to expensive dinners, buy her stuff and have babies with her?

Studies have also determined that once a man enters into a relationship and falls in love, his testosterone levels drop and he becomes "beta-ized". In other words, his body recognizes the potential for upcoming offspring with a trusted partner and flips the provider switch *for* him, thus making him a better nurturer.

….Sounds enticing, no?

I'm just teasing of course. The point is this: make your role clear. Keep asking yourself what you want and stay true to it. Let me tell you, staying true to what you want when you have a strong emotional bond to a woman and she's pushing your buttons is HARD. You will falter, you will feel like crap, and you will learn from it and come out a better man.

On Sexuality

There are whole books on lovemaking and sexuality, so I'll keep this section short and limited to just a handful of my most profound realizations about sex:

1. Whatever Happens Is OK

Whether you know it or not, there are a lot of expectations that are thrust upon men in regards to their sexuality. Perhaps not as much as women, but men have their own bag.

For one, men are expected to be always sexually 'ready'. Compared to women, men actually have a very small sexual capacity. A man can have an orgasm, perhaps a handful. And each subsequent orgasm weakens in intensity. A woman can go on having orgasm after orgasm and the intensity only grows.

It's important to also understand that man is an animal and no animal is in heat all year round. Sexuality is cyclical, rhythmic. It varies depending upon many, many things like mood, work life, exercise, diet, weather, and many other factors.

Yet many guys expect themselves to be horny all the time. And some are. But some aren't. And most are in between. Many women also have the mistaken idea that a guy should be 'standing at attention' 24/7. This expectation leads to disappointments in the bedroom and unnecessary feelings of inadequacy and shame for the man.

Drop expectations in the bedroom. Of yourself and of your lover. Nothing is "supposed" to happen in there. You can make love, you can talk, you can fool around, you can play fight, you can do whatever feels good to you both, and it's all good. There's no need to force anything. In fact, the more you try to force, the less enjoyable it is.

Whatever happens is OK.

2. Sex Is Play

To make sex more enjoyable, it helps to treat it as play. Don't make it into a serious affair. There's enough seriousness in both of your lives. Sex is a frolicking in the rolling grass, under fragrant trees.

If you cum, great. If she cums, great. If neither of you cum, great. If she cums twice and you don't cum at all, awesome. It's ALL good! Sex isn't work yet it's easy to get into a goal-oriented frame of mind where you think "I have to make X, Y and Z happen."

It satisfies the ego to chase goals because you can call yourself a great lover when you 'accomplish' them. The flip side is that you will call yourself a poor lover when you *don't* accomplish them. And since many of these goals come from unrealistic expectations about what should happen in between the sheets, it's more likely that you'll make yourself miserable with your sexual ambitions.

In fact, the whole thing puts a lot of pressure on you and you can easily get caught up in performance anxiety and bog down the lightheartedness of it all. It also puts pressure on the woman you're with because she can feel your tension and your mind working and it's going to put her on edge as well. She will even likely think that it has something to do with her attractiveness or lack thereof.

When you're coming from a place of playfulness, sex is more fun and enjoyable. Expectations are far away. You're in the moment. You're in your bodies and out of your heads. You're playing!

3. Communicate

It can be difficult at first to communicate what you want in bed. It's a sensitive topic for a woman in particular because any 'coaching' you give can easily make her feel inadequate. After all, if she knew what she was doing and pleasuring you well, she wouldn't need any tips, *right?* Well, not quite... Nobody is **born** a great lover. We all know how to put it in (and even that can be surprisingly complicated) but there's more to love making than merely putting it in.

So if your gal is going down on you, for instance, and it doesn't feel good, gently and lovingly adjust her hands or mouth and tell her what you'd like her to do. Give her feedback about what feels good to you. Make it specific so she can actually learn something from the experience.

She might bristle a little at first because she's in a very vulnerable position emotionally. Here she is worshipping your member and you're telling her that she's not doing a good job. At least that's what it feels like to her. *So approach it lovingly.* She'll appreciate your communicativeness and you'll both have better sex because of it.

4. Watch Each Other Masturbate

Nobody knows how to please you better than you. Likewise for your lover. It's good to watch the other playing with themselves and masturbating a little so you can see what the person is doing. There's a lot of nuance to the way a person likes to cum.

There are things to consider on both sides like pressure, firmness, grip, suction, pacing, rhythm, speed, the build up, breathing. It's a very subtle and symphonic thing to see the way a person moves into and out of orgasm.

I'm not saying to set up a mutual masturbation date or anything. But when you're in bed and touching yourselves and your girl is playing with herself a little, just watch her, encourage her gently, tell her how it turns you on. And pay close attention to what she's doing. Think about it...she's giving you the key to getting her off exactly the way she likes it.

5. Slow Down

Most lovemaking is way too rushed. Ask women, they'll tell you the same thing. All of the porn out there and the ideas about sex we're exposed to suggest that sex consists of jumping headlong into full-blown humping. And that has it's place of course.

But in general ...what's the hurry?! Sex isn't some action-item on your to do list in between the gym and beers with the fellas. It's a goal-less play. Sex can be a pop song or a symphony. Your gal will be much more turned on if you slowly build up the suspense. If you take the time to turn her on, tease her a bit and get her rearing to go so she's dripping wet by the time you enter her.

By the time most men are finishing, a woman is only beginning. So slow it down. Just try a different pacing from time to time and see how it feels. You might be surprised to see that you enjoy it more as well.

6. Breathe

Remember. To. Breathe...

The State of Being Good With Women

There is no resting state in any life process. All of existence is continually changing, evolving, growing. Your knowledge is always incomplete and amenable. At best, you can say you have *a pretty good idea of what seems to be the case at the moment, based on the information that you have and assuming the information is accurate...* Beyond that, you're shooting in the dark.

But science has shown that life is in a state of flux. Species are constantly changing, morphing, evolving. If existence is evolving, that means that it is incomplete. Completion means a stoppage, a final rest. But no such rest exists. In this life, there is no completion. You aren't in the state of 'having been' just because yesterday is gone. You are in a state of 'being' because now is going...

The implication of this idea is that God created an imperfect universe. And the implication of **that** implication is that God must be a fraud. How could somebody all powerful, all knowing and perfect in every way, create something *im*perfect? He must not exist...

But God DOES exist! ...Just not in the form of some divine dude in the clouds. God IS the clouds. God is the moon. God is you, god is me. God is a beautiful woman sauntering down the street, and God is the street, itself.

Through the belief in 'a God', we divorce ourselves from the totality of existence and our place in it. By joining in existence *itself*, you find God... And no belief is necessary because your experience of God, divinity, holiness - is here on Earth. You only need belief for things that don't exist. Otherwise, you'd be able to touch god. You'd be able to smell god in a glass of Malbec. You'd taste god on the lips of your lover. You'd feel god beating inside your chest when you go for a run.

Just as the separation between mind and body is arbitrary, so too is the separation between matter and spirit. This is one existence. You are in it. You are part of it. You've always been part of it, and you'll always remain part of it.

And in fact, you've already had these moments of religiousness. Perhaps during an orgasm, or a silent day at the lake, or an eternal moment when you were strumming on your guitar with such absorption that you forgot where you were, who you were and even THAT you were. And in that forgetting, the stream of your being flowed into the river of all things.

And you'll find that you never really 'get good' with women. Because that would mean your learning, your growing and evolving is over. And the more you glimpse the mystery of woman, the more you laugh at the idea of ever understanding her in all her glory…

Mutual Freedom

Women never cheat on me. And I never cheat on women. For the simple reason that I make it clear from the get-go that I follow my heart no matter what. If my heart leads me to move with another woman, I do it. And should the gal I'm with wish to flow with another man, it's not my place to stop her and none of my business to inquire about it.

This is mutual freedom and it isn't for everybody. It can't be for everybody because it takes guts. And not everybody has guts. To have guts means that you are secure enough in your value as a human being, that should a woman you're 'with' go and play the field, she'll still be able to come back to you without you judging, shaming or belittling her. Or making her feel bad that she's enjoying her life with other men when she's not with you.

It also means that you never trade your freedom to be yourselves for a false sense of security and togetherness. That's the whole rotten role of "relationships". They should disappear from the earth. Once relating has stopped and a relationship is put in its place, patterns and expectations and obligations set in and things are bound to fall flat.

To have guts also means having the courage to let a lover go or walk away gracefully when the love has run its course. Love, contrary to everything you've been told, is NOT eternal. It cannot be 'forever' or fixed, because life is flux, life is flow, life is change. The way you feel about somebody will always go on changing. That's the way of existence. To cling to it, to cage it with words like 'boyfriend' and 'girlfriend', 'husband' and 'wife', is foolishness. Love comes and goes. And once it goes, have the guts to move on, for both of your sakes.

The Courage To Love Who You Love

Liking who you like and loving who you love takes a lot of courage. Because you've been stuffed full of ideas about what is beautiful, what is sexy, what is feminine.

And if you meet a woman and fall in love with her and she doesn't conform to these ideas, you come into difficulty. After all, you feel something undeniable in your heart. A resonance. A polarity. A chemistry. But your head won't give you peace! You *feel* that she is beautiful but you look at her and you look at the picture of the girl in the magazine and suddenly you're not so sure. You feel that she is a rare and unique flower yet you see how women behave on television and she doesn't quite fit the mold. And you feel again that you're not so sure...

The only beacon you have to guide you is the light of your own heart. If everybody is telling you that she is bad but you know she is good, you say "I don't care! I love her." If everybody is telling you she is ugly, you look at her with your own two eyes and see whether you feel it to really be true.

The average man moves with a hot woman whom he can't stand on a personal level because it lets *other* men know that he's capable of attracting hot women. It's just like a child tugging on his daddy's pant legs, saying "look at me! Look what I can do!" But she is only hot, she's not beautiful. And she is merely the instrument he uses to bolster his reflected sense of self-worth.

A superficial man moves with superficial women. But a centered man looks at a woman's core. Of course, no man can deny that physical attractiveness is important. It's requisite. But it's just the minimum. With hotness you will soon be bored and you will start looking for something deeper. And then you will find beauty. And in earnestly searching for beauty, hotness starts to surround you as well. It's the strangest thing...

Directness And Intention

Real men are open and direct about their intentions, yet totally respectful. This applies in business, in friendships, in love.

With lovers for instance, a direct man is not presumptuous but **curious**. Curious as to who this woman before him IS and what kinds of surprises the interaction has in store for him.

The problem is: *men today are afraid to offend.* They beat around the bush, skirt issues that are obviously on their minds and avoid saying what they're *really* thinking at all costs. This is a symptom of the real root cause - **inauthenticity**.

You are taught and conditioned in every possible way to avoid being yourself. You are taught comparison to others and competition with others. you look into another man's pocket, onto his resume and even into his bed, to see how you stack up.

And you can NEVER be satisfied. Because *your* achievements will always be overshadowed by another. Another man's girlfriend is hotter than yours. Another man makes more money. Another man has bigger muscles and drives a nicer car. And you are taught to look at everybody ELSE and measure your worth according to *them*.

Do you see how cunning this manipulation is? How can you EVER make more money or be more handsome or have more women than another man? There will ALWAYS be somebody to outdo you. Always. Not just one man, but thousands upon thousands! It's never ending. Somebody will always come around to one-up you, to make you feel inadequate.

It's time to stop looking at everybody *else* and start looking within yourself. It's time to become a light unto yourself, unconcerned with the brightness of another man's light. Instead of asking "how do I compare?" ask "am I doing what I want?", "am I following my heart?"

It will take some practice. Your conditioning to compare is SO strong that even as you recognize and feel its absurdity, you continue to do it. Can you say that the rose is more beautiful than the lily? Can you say that the sun is better than the moon or the ocean superior to the land?

You are a totally unique individual and comparison with others is not only absurd ...it's fundamentally impossible! It is your society's *trick* to keep you in a feeling of inadequacy and discontentment. Because in this state, you desperately struggle to ascend higher and higher on the career ladder, to earn more and more money, more and more prestige, more approval, more respect. More, more, more.

Yet somehow ...it never feels like enough. You always feel *just shy* of 'true' success. Just a dollar short of being truly rich. Just a shag away from being a *true* ladies man. Just 10 pounds away from being a true stud on the benchpress. There's still SO much to be accomplished, to be proven to your friends and family that YES, you are a success. You really ARE 'good enough.' And finally, truly, really, and forevermore, you are a REAL man!

But... this isn't the path to manhood. It's the path to hamsterhood. You can run on the hamster wheel with all your might but you'll die before you get anywhere worth going...

How To Drop The Crap

A little understanding will go a long way here. The fundamental problem keeping you from a life of happiness and overflowingness is the ego.

The ego is a substitute self. It works like this: As a child your parents begin to praise you. For instance, they praise you for doing well in school. They tell you how smart you are, what a good boy you are. Then one day you get a report card with poor grades. Now your parents withdraw affection. All of a sudden, you're no longer a 'good boy', or a 'smart boy.' "Why", they ask, "can't you be more like the neighbor boy, who always gets the highest grade?" They introduce comparison and competition into your heart. You, yourself, are no longer the yardstick of your own life. *You now feel relative to every other boy*. Envy and jealousy inevitably creep into your inner ecology. And you make a habit out of always comparing.

You thought your parents cared about you but they seem now to be angry with you that you didn't behave up to *their* standard. You thought their love was unconditional but now you've had your first taste of emotional blackmail. You feel betrayed, jaded. How could your parents do this to you? Don't they have enough respect for you to let you find your own way? No, they force a way on you because THEY know best. You don't know. You're too young and stupid and incapable of figuring it out on your own. You need to be kept on a short leash...

And this is why the vast majority of children can never forgive their parents. They have suffocated you and stunted your growth. And when you reach adulthood, you are a crippled man who must now find ways to uncripple himself.

...**Of course, this is just an example** and I've hyperbolized to make it the concept more obvious. There are a million variations on this theme.

Whether they know it or not, the parents are creating an ego in you. A pride that is dependent always on an outside source. When you feed it with praise, approval and attention, it swells. When you deprive it of these things, it aches.

You start to question your own personal mythology. That maybe you're AREN'T so smart after all. Maybe you aren't a good boy, but a rotten boy. To face such an idea would mean facing the truth: that your parents lied to you, manipulated you and created an *idea of you* for their own gain, which you now cling to in lieu of the *real you*.

But it's easier to believe something about yourself that OTHERS have told you, than to find out who you *really* are and what you really want. Perhaps the boy in our example started to hate school because he intuited, even at such a tender age, that his tyrannical teachers have no business handling young minds. And the curriculum is set up to cater to the dullest students, of whom he is not one. So rather than sit in class and sniff glue just to cope with the boredom, he prefers to play hookie and go to the playground.

Have you noticed how easy it is to flatter an egotistical person? An egotist swells when others notice their wonderful attributes. It allows them to believe they're wonderful. But it's a trap because it comes from others. It must come from you. And you may be surprised to discover just how many of your behaviors exist merely to garner approval/attention/praise, and how many exist to prevent *dis*approval and the ***withdrawal*** of praise. In essence, you are doing these things for other people.

The guy who brags to his buddies about his sexual conquests is inflating his ego at the expense of the girls he's slept with. And no matter how much he "achieves" in that department and no matter how much approbation his friends lavish on him, he always feels strangely deflated after sharing...

Because the ego is a black hole. Whatsoever you throw into it disappears. There is no satisfying it. *So how you drop it?* You don't. Let this be understood: **You can't fight the ego directly.** It's like darkness. Darkness has no positive existence. It is simply the absence of light. You don't take away the darkness. If you want no more darkness, you must introduce the light.
Same with the ego. You can't drop it or fight it or struggle against it. This is futile. It's a part of you and a part of your psychology. You can, however, keep it from terrorizing you and the people in your life. *And you do this by watching it.*

Watchfulness is a concept that's been around for thousands of years in the Eastern religions, whose very goal has been to enter into a blissful, egoless state. The East has dedicated the majority of its genius to exploring the inner world and developing inner technologies to live happily, here and now. The West has poured its brilliance into material development. So now, a strange dilemma exists. The people of the East are rich in spirituality but many live in great poverty. The people of the West are materially wealthy but feel as though their lives are utterly meaningless...

The technique is this: simply watch, notice, observe - EVERYTHING - that comes and goes within your being. Whether you feel angry or sad or happy or jealous or nervous – it doesn't matter. You watch it all. Just watch...

And even though most of the West looks at Eastern concepts of spirituality with a certain scorn and skepticism, Western psychiatrists have arrived at a phenomenon called "observing ego", which is the scientifically proven equivalent of watchfulness. Aha. So it's real, proven and it works. Play with it and give it a bit of time. It may just change your life completely...

Meditation

The mature man is necessarily meditative.

Mature women move with mature men and vice versa. Mature men befriend other mature men. And in meditation you ripen, you mature. Meditation is simply what happens when you watch all things, inside of you and outside of you.

Simply watching without any interpretation on the part of your mind. Watching like a man sitting on the bank of a river, seeing the water flow. The water flows. What possible interpretation could there be?

Meditation is the art of opening your eyes. It's the acceptance of things <u>as they are</u> without labels of good, bad, right, wrong, etc. A woman wants to be able to act tempestuously and impulsively around a man, and feel secure that he won't judge her, think less of her or let her behavior rock him off his center. And your center grows in meditation.

Meditation is a very practical thing. You don't need to sit in a lotus position and repeat a mantra. Nor do you need to *believe* in it. It's not a doctrine or a philosophy so it requires no faith or belief. It's a real life, existential phenomenon. So all you have to do is try it for yourself and you'll see first hand its value.

In order for you to come into full flowering as a man, meditation is necessary. For the simple reason that real men are creators. To create requires dissolving the conditioning and borrowed knowledge that has been forced upon you and moving into a place of innocence, curiosity, joy and marveling. In meditation, these artificial structures melt away...

With your growing meditativeness, you'll begin to notice a distance being created between that which happens and the way you respond.

Most people don't respond, they react. Somebody says something to you and it pisses you off. You get angry. **You become the anger.** You are identified with it. You react out of your anger or you fight the feeling and repress it, which only increases your misery. Either way, the external situation drives and controls you. You may react with it or against it, but in both cases the anger rules you.

A girl turns her nose up at you, and you feel humiliated, that "who does she think she is, to act in such a way towards me...?"

Play with a new approach... The approach is to watch. To notice, to witness what is happening. Simply watch the situation, watch the emotions that arise in you. Just watch. Your mind will be frantically labeling things as 'good', 'bad', 'annoying', 'pleasant'. Watch these thoughts too.

As you watch, you'll notice your mind quieting down. In that space, you will have the breathing room to see a situation for what it is. You'll have the space to *choose* your response. Since a choice is involved, you're not reacting. You are responding. And because you are watching yourself, you will also come to realize that you are not the doer. **You are the watcher.** *Otherwise, WHO is watching the doer...?*

You will see how feelings and situations come and go like monsoon rains. One minute it's sunny and hot. The next minute it's raining violently. But YOU are not the rain. You are not the heat.

This is the true meaning of the word responsibility. It is simply your ability to respond to a situation with awareness and clarity. So it's really a beautiful word because it means you can move through life and choose your path. You can create your life afresh, anew, every single day. And you can drop your knee-jerk reactivity to others, which is a form of slavery.

But the word responsibility has been corrupted to mean duty. Duty to your country. Duty to your religion. Duty to your family. Duty to your children. But duty means you act in a prescribed way. The prescription absolves you of the need to stay aware, and dulls your intelligence.

True responsibility is a blessing, a gift to yourself and to those around. It is a catalyst for manhood. And it arises from your meditativeness. In fact, meditation is almost magical. Because many of the qualities that make a man into a **real man** grow and thrive in meditation. It is a transformative state in which existence flows through you and imparts to you its infiniteness...

On Stoicism

Many men erroneously believe that it is unmanly and unbecoming to experience or display strong emotions. "We must be STOIC!" we're told.

But men are not unemotional creatures. We are, in our own way, just as emotional as women. To be emotional simply means to have the capacity to experience emotion. *So what's the problem?* The problem arises when an emotion grows so intense that it blinds you to all reason and prevents any possibility of awareness and sensitivity in a situation. So it's not emotion *per se* that creates the problems, it is too much of it.

Many men have the idea that to feel emotion is somehow 'effeminate', which violates their idea of rock-like masculinity. This stings the ego. Because it must mean that whenever you feel emotional, you're not a REAL man. You're displaying a supposedly female trait, so you must be effeminate and less of a man. So you vainly repress and fight with your emotions and overcompensate with exaggerated 'manhood'. *But this is a dead end road.*

Repressing emotions is incredibly dangerous to emotional, psychological and even physical well being. Not only that, but repression is a futile battle. Repressed emotions <u>always</u> percolate back to the top of consciousness sooner or later. And they resurface in grotesque incarnations.

The word 'emotion' is significant... It means to 'move out'. That which moves within you and out of you is *alive*. So emotions indicate your aliveness. The unemotional person is unalive. And a dead man is compelling to nobody, least of all to a woman. But because emotions move out, you can always count on them passing like clouds in the sky.

Sometimes the sky is clear and sunny. Other days it's drizzling. Some days it's partly cloudy and every so often, a thunderstorm blasts through. You may even get the feeling that this storm will rage forever, even though you know perfectly well that all storms pass... The key is to watch these emotions with curiosity and a deep trust they will go, just as they came. And they will.

Nor is emotion somehow opposed to reason. They are not opposites but complimentaries. It is not illogical to be emotional. That, in itself, would be illogical. Because reason depends on assessing the facts of reality as they are and drawing the conclusions from them. And what IS, is that you are emoting. To be a strong communicator, particularly in the language of the heart, you'll need to be emotive. To express yourself clearly and honestly.

So the split between reason and emotion is arbitrary. They are two sides of the same coin, which is your ability respond, think and act intelligently...

The Hormonal Component

There's an undeniable hormonal component to manhood. Healthy, fit men have higher testosterone levels (as well as other androgens) and as a result, experience better well being, higher sex drives, more aggressiveness and other biologically 'masculine' attributes.

Eating well, working out, getting sunshine, getting adequate sleep, and keeping stress low all contribute greatly to a feeling of zest and vigor. If you ignore this part of your life, you'll be missing a vital and *visceral* component of manhood.

Your body is your temple. *Does your temple inspire people to come and have a moment of religiousness at the altar...?* Do you look at yourself with disgust or with pride? Do you feel energetic, healthy and vibrant? Or lackluster, lackadaisical and sluggish? Before you're a man, you're a human being. And before that, you're an animal. And like any animal, you need health to be vigorous. Health is the foundation, the bedrock. It's important. Don't ignore it...

However, the conventional advice around nutrition, sleep, stress management and exercise is totally whack. I highly recommend you check out Mark Sisson's book **"The Primal Blueprint"** to get on the right track from the very beginning. (I have *zero* affiliation with Mark)

Aloneness vs Loneliness

There's a difference between loneliness and aloneness. Loneliness is a feeling that you NEED others, that without others your sense of self is uncertain. Aloneness is different. To be alone means to go deep into your inner world and spend time with yourself. Even though we all need companionship, socialization and camaraderie, aloneness is needed too. Because they're really two sides of the same coin.

To spend time alone with yourself means to get to know yourself more intimately. Subsequently, when you go out into the world, you are better able to relate with other people at their centers, because you are at *your* center.

You can be alone but feel a great connectedness with the rest of the world and with humanity. On the other hand, you can spend all of your time in the company of others yet feel utterly alone in the universe. That's because the fundamental requirement to relate with other people is to first relate with your own self.

When you *have* your self, *know* yourself and are committed to *being* yourself, you're able to walk into any situation confidently. You'll be confident because you'll know, that no matter what existence presents you with, you can count on you to be you.

So in fact, aloneness is **necessary** to be able to relate with others candidly, compellingly, completely. Otherwise, if you haven't yet found yourself, WHO will be there to relate with another? The center relates to the other center. The periphery relates to the other periphery. A compelling man touches those around him at their very centers. *He makes people feel visible.* He penetrates the periphery because it's boring, superficial and only momentarily interesting - and goes right to the core. He is coming from his center so he looks to relate to the center of the other.

A Man of Action

Men of action are a dying breed. We live in the information age and man uses his mind to earn a living more and more, and uses his hands less and less. But whatever the reasons, man is more in his head than ever, and less in his body.

Yet *everything* is the result of action. Thought is good. Foresight is good. But wrong action is better than protracted, right thinking. The latter can become mental masturbation. And it often does.

Why is it important to be a man of action? Because action creates. With your physical movement through the world, by putting your hands upon life and literally touching it, handling it, manipulating it, you undertake an act of great creativity.

Action is the force that brings about the kind of life you dream of, only not in the dream world but in real life. By taking action towards the things you want no matter how scared or uncertain you are, you automatically grow as a man.

So real manhood is in your hands. Simply pick it up, sling it over your shoulder, and walk into the unknown with all of your strength and awareness.

To Many Bold Adventures...
Vincent Vinturi

A Word From Vincent:

If you enjoyed this read, please stop by the Amazon page and take a second to leave your <u>honest</u> feedback.

It would mean the world to me and potential readers to hear *your* thoughts. Here's the link:

<u>http://www.RealNaturalSeduction.com/manhood-book</u>